CHRISTIANITY

vs

Islam

CHRISTIANITY
VS
Islam

The Honorable Elijah Muhammad
MESSENGER OF ALLAH

A
SECRETARIUS PUBLICATION

Dedicated to
the doers
of the
Word...

CHRISTIANITY vs ISLAM

First Edition Released 1993
Revised/Second Printing 1994
Third Printing 1997

Published by
**MESSENGER ELIJAH MUHAMMAD
PROPAGATION SOCIETY
(M.E.M.P.S.)**

P.O. BOX 162412 • ATLANTA, GA 30321

**FOR 24HR
RETAIL CATALOG & WHOLESALE INFORMATION
770 907-2212**

ISBN # 1-884855-03-2

Contents

Acknowledgements *iv*
Introduction *v*

The History of Two Worlds
Chapter 1 **1**

The Tribe of Shabazz
Chapter 2 **5**

Blackman and Adam
Chapter 3 **11**

The Making of the Moon
Chapter 4 **14**

Atomic Bombs to Fight Allah
Chapter 5 **17**

Origin of the White Race - Devils
Chapter 6 **19**

The Judgement of the World
Chapter 7 **26**

Contents Continued . . .

Jesus: Only A Prophet
Chapter 8 29

The Resurrection and the Hereafter
Chapter 9 33

Curse of Yakub's Civilization
Chapter 10 37

The Slave-Master and His Religion
Chapter 11 44

Separation: Not Integration
Chapter 12 48

. . . And This Is Christianity
Chapter 13 52

The Crescent And The Cross
Chapter 14 58

Persecution Follows Coming of God
Closing Note 63

❖ ❖ ❖ ❖ ❖

The Following Book Was
Transcribed From A Lecture
Given By The Honorable
Elijah Muhammad,
Messenger of Allah, on
November 7, 1962,
Philadelphia, Penn.

❖ ❖ ❖ ❖ ❖ ❖

The Audio Version Is
Also Available By
Contacting The Publisher,
SECRETARIUS.

Acknowledgments

"Whoever brings a good deed will have tenfold like it . . ." (Holy Qur'an 6:161)

"And judging on that day will be just; so as for those whose good deeds are heavy, they are the successful." (Holy Qur'an 7:8)

I thank Allah (God), Master Fard Muhammad, for the mental capacity and desire to contribute to the great work of delivering the Words He had given to His Last and Greatest Messenger, The Honorable Elijah Muhammad.

The making of this transcripted book of the Honorable Elijah Muhammad was a task made much easier by the assistance given by Azzam Waathiq Basir, Rose Hakim, Dur're Shahwar Aqeela bint Hakim, Taqqee Aamil Hakim, Junaid Shafeeq Hakim and Khalfani Hassan Hakim, who comprise the Secretarius Staff. Thank you all and may Allah continue to bless you.

Minister Nasir Makr Hakim
C.E.O. Secretarius

Introduction

Christianity versus Islam, as this book is so titled, is more so a comparative study rather than a challenge of one to the other. And since one of many primary principles of Islam is that it's adherents are to never be the aggressor; thus the book's title is Christianity versus Islam instead of Islam versus Christianity.

When studying the works of the Honorable Elijah Muhammad, Messenger of Allah, one sees in Message To The Blackman In America, a major book written by the Messenger, that within the first two chapters, he deals with the subject of if God is a spirit and the reader's basis for believing such. The first example he cites is the basic pillars of Christianity: The belief that God is a spirit with a flesh and blood son, and a Ghost and that the three are equally God. The Messenger uses mathematics and nature as a basis to refute this type of belief.

What we must keep in mind is the name of the first two chapters in Message To The Blackman, and that is "Allah Is God. Who Is That Mystery God?"

The Messenger unequivocally states that God is a Man and not a spirit. It is no doubt that his teachings not only challenges the common man's beliefs, but rocks the basis of belief that the whole world rests on. Such truths challenge any teachings which has as its base a spirit for its God; therefore, Christendom alone isn't singled out per say, but any body of knowledge that operates while resting on an adherence to the unknown.

"The belief in a God other than man (a spirit), Allah has taught me, goes back into the millions of years - long before Yakub (the father of the devils) - because the knowledge of God was kept as a secret from the public. This is the first time that it has ever been revealed, and we, the poor rejected and despised people, are blessed to be the first of all the people of earth to receive this secret knowledge of God. If this people (the white race) would teach you truth which has been revealed to me, they would be hastening their own doom - for they were not created to teach us the truth, but rather to teach us falsehood (just contrary to the truth)." (Message To The Blackman In America, by The Honorable Elijah Muhammad, pg. 9)

If a belief of God being other than man "goes back into the millions of years," then it couldn't have been called Christianity; for organized Christianity, as we know it, is only approximately 615 years old; therefore, we're left with the understanding that it's not just the label, but more importantly, the mind set. If we examine this closely, all religions that believe that a spirit God is at its base can just as easily be classified in the same category as Christianity.

The lecture which has been transcribed into this book deals with the two aspects which are classified as two worlds: one believing in the reality of God, with God being a real entity Himself-a Man, and secondly, a make believe world with a non-tangible God, with no proof of its existence, and its worshippers believing in what they know not what.

As a result of Black people in America not having the right knowledge of self and the world around us, we have accepted many versions of our identity; consequently, we have been in a state of confusion which spreads from one generation to another. It was the Honorable Elijah Muhammad who pierced through this veil of confusion and pointed out irrefutable actual facts pertaining to who we are, because God Himself taught him. He wasn't just given truths without iron clad support from scripture and that which is based on the natural laws of this universe.

Never before has anyone taught efficiently about the Moon and its sciences and how we, black people, were tied to it and the fact that it was our tribe, the God Tribe of Shabazz, who resettled the planet after the blasting away of the moon from the planet we now live on. Out of what lodge, church, night club, or meeting hall have you and I been given this vast wisdom before the Honorable Elijah Muhammad, Messenger of Allah?

The depth of this wisdom touches whites too, because before the Honorable Elijah Muhammad, they had an identity problem too. While reflecting on one of the Theology of Time Lectures of the Messenger, he was discussing a dialogue which he and a preacher had regarding the teachings and the Messenger said, "We had it going for a while there until my fire out burned his, and he said, 'they just don't give us that over there,' I told him that they don't have that to give you." This is exactly why the Messenger would state that if he let the devil (whites) in the meetings that there wouldn't be standing room. The devil understands the value of these teachings more than we do. He is thirsting for the knowledge of himself too.

The two worlds are at a showdown now and all must be separated onto their own kind. In this time of religious, political, ethnic, cultural and ideological integration, Almighty God has missioned His Messenger, Elijah Muhammad, to trumpet the message of separation which is equal in appearance to an ark on dry land. It is deemed political suicide to advocate such, especially in America.

To accept, practice and advocate separation in this day, one would deem you either dangerously serious or crazy, but was this not what those with Noah had to go through. As God tested them then, so are we today.

Like yesterday in Noah's time, the disbelievers of Jesus' time didn't believe either; however, they went a step further. They chose to deify Jesus and say he was God's son and in light of the people being without the knowledge of the reality or person of God, once again they started worshipping their own ideas. "Christ" became a buzz word for the type of teachings whites began to use on the darker peoples of the earth for the purpose of enslaving them; for as the Messenger stated, "This teaching of a mystery God enslaves the minds of the ignorant."

The most ignorant of the people today are those who were of the tribe of Shabazz who strayed away from civilization approximately 50,000 years ago, so teaches the Honorable Elijah Muhammad. And as a result of straying so far away, they began living a jungle existence.

It was 50,000 years ago when we suffered our complete fall. Being in this condition of being unaware of what was taking place on a global level, through the whites global explorations, they found us living in peaceful circumstances, unaware of the evil potential these new visitor posed.

Being without the knowledge of them, we were vulnerable to their tricks, lies and power; consequently, we fell victim. Upon being kidnapped and taken to various parts of the planet for slave labor purposes, we ultimately were mentally killed, meaning, we were robbed of the knowledge of knowing that we were even human and our whole existence was redefined by these enemies of ours. We were taught that we were made from serving whites and the "Christian" religion supported and recommended it. It is highly interesting when looking at the name of the man whom the western world says discovered America, its etymological roots enlightens us: Christopher = Christ - opher. "opher" means bearer and this feeds back into the buzz word concept mentioned previously that it was the exportation of a mind set which in essence is designed to conquer aboriginals of the earth, in the name of "Jesus Christ."

The whites know there is no spirit Jesus or a mystery God, but they know that you and I don't know; therefore, the trick is to make you think there is one and that they are the speakers and interpreters of "His Words." This is what made a "White Jesus" suitable for the purpose of imagery: To help support the thought they had planted.

Rendered in this condition of mental and physical slavery, and being deprived of all knowledge of self, we were considered mentally dead, because we didn't know self, nor any one else and thereby assumed the existence of a beast of the field and were treated accordingly as chattel. The Messenger teaches us that if Christianity was a wet rag and you rung it out, every drop would spell slavery for the Blackman and Woman.

Regardless of how long this trick has been going on, that does not take away from the prophesies of the prophets; wherein, they all talked about a time when God Himself would come and raise the dead, not the physically dead, but the mental dead. And from that mentally dead, He would raise One whose mission it would be to teach the rest. The first one would be considered God's First Born, and spiritually, the Son of God. When we read this symbolically written in scripture, it's told to us under the story of Jesus of 2,000 years ago. One symbol of Jesus is that He raised the dead and another tells us that he rose from the dead. Both of these things have occurred, but by two different men who fulfilled these prophesies. It was Master Fard Muhammad, Allah (God), the "Jesus" Who RAISED the mental dead (Lazarus), and it was the Honorable Elijah Muhammad, the "Jesus" who rose from the mentally dead. God's spiritual Son, His First Born.

Today the Honorable Elijah Muhammad's teachings are the most powerful on this planet. This has already been proven by the work that has been demonstrated; for when we reflect on the condition of the people that's in question and the state they were in: A state of mental death, not even knowing that they were human and living the life of beast as a result of being thoroughly robbed of the knowledge of themselves and others by their slave-masters and children, no where in history is there history of a people brought from this state and raised to a living perpendicular and equipped with the capacity to rule this world and build one better.

The power is with God, Master Fard Muhammad, the God Who the Honorable Elijah Muhammad represented to us and the God Who is the sole teacher of the Messenger and Author of what he teaches, none other. The greatest and only legacy which the Messenger had is that what he teaches and taught came from only ONE MAN: ALLAH (GOD), WHO CAME IN THE PERSON OF MASTER FARD MUHAMMAD. Many would like to steal a share, or simply subscribe to schools of thought which advocates a share in the Messengers teachings and program, and this couldn't be further from the truth and facts, as the old saying goes: Success is an orphan with man fathers.

There is a final struggle taking place, and that is between the two worlds spoken of. There are armies gathering together for the doom of this world as we know it and a new world is coming into being. After this war, it won't be like those of old when the white race divided the spoils and go back to business as usual; there is going to be a total destruction of their world.

As formally seen in the temples in the earlier days, a Actual Facts Board with the Holy Universe Flag of Islam and the flag of America on the black board, with the words in between: Which One Will Survive The War Of Armageddon? There will be no winners and losers, per say, which is why that question is put forth as it is: Which one will survive?

You and I know that there is nothing that can out-last the Sun, Moon and Star. We all need them regardless of what we believe in presently and if it were not for them, we would not have a universe in the first place. The Sun, Moon and Star are the symbols for Islam, because it is the Nature of God. How could God give you and I anything other than that, and it would also stand to reason that He would not have given anything other than that; therefore, it there stands before us another type of world, it couldn't be from the Creator of this universe!

This book will open the eyes of all who read it regardless of our persuasion and walk of life. This knowledge is absolutely necessary to many the critical decisions we all need to make in this final hour.

Minister Nasir Makr Hakim
C.E.O., Secretarius

CHAPTER 1

The History Of Two Worlds

As-Salaam Alaikum

To you who have arrived here at this particular address to hear this subject, Christianity versus Islam, I thank you, and I feel more than honored at your presence here this afternoon. And I thank each and every one of you whether you are a common laborer, whether you are blind, deaf and dumb or whether you are a professor of a college or a university. I thank you for you presence here this afternoon.

We the Muslims greet you As-Salaam-Alaikum which means peace be unto you. This is an Arab word for peace. In going after this subject this afternoon, we must remember whether or not there is time for such understanding - or we will just say - a show down between the two religions. If it's not time we [will] not be successful in trying to make you understand the truth and if this is the time, we will know by your understanding and we will know by your actions or reactions to the truth.

We may sum up a few events of the past, we take back 6,000 years ago according to the word of Almighty God Allah when this world was being fashioned, the white man's world, we have on the pages of history, much confusion, much conflict between Islam or the Muslims, are the builders or manufacturers of this world. We have arrived now at the day we call 6,000 years from the creation of the white man's world. And according to the prophecy, according to your own understanding of the history, the truth must be told. I hope that I don't irritate you; truth is a little thing that hurts. I didn't come out here to dominate your religion nor anyone's religion, I'm here to tell the truth.

We have lived under the whiteman's rule for now, 6,000 years: Six days they work and on the seventh day rest. We are in the day of rest of their world, and you are surprised. Some of you are confused over what is taking place. But a knowledge of the history of this world and the prophecy explaining the ending of this world, you should not be surprised. Some of us have been so surprised that we go astray and exaggerate, heading in and out of the truth.

The so-called American Negro, who is not a Negro, but a slave name given to them by their slave-master, who had no love nor friendship for them, and after making them blind deaf and dumb to the knowledge of themselves, they called them negroes, which means something that is dead, lifeless, neutral; in words to say: that here stands a man that [has] no knowledge of himself and he's neutral, he's not one of us, nor is he one of their own kind, and that he's like something that is dead that you go take it and place it over here, sit it down or stand it up, it will remain in the position you put it in until you change that position.

These people have been mistreated by their slave-masters and the slave masters' children worst than any human being or beings that ever was on our planet earth according to history. We have suffered all kinds of cruelty, beatings, and murder, all the days since we have been in the Western Hemisphere; it's going on right at this hour. And today, truth must be told and the truth will free that man of his ignorant knowledge of his master and of himself.

I want you to remember again, that this subject, the two religions, it's not that I want you to go down on your knees and start praying this afternoon looking in the skies, no, I'm not actually teaching too much religion, because how can you learn religion unless you first learn yourself. Our people are so sold to religion; why, because they are the people of the divine family.

CHAPTER 2

THE TRIBE OF SHABAZZ

The so-called American Negros [are] members of the Tribe of Shabazz. Shabazz was a scientist that went into what was then known as the jungle of East Asia, according to the teachings of Almighty God, Allah to me. Fifty thousand (50,000) years ago, he started with his family there in what you call today the jungles of Africa. There he taken his family and he started a civilization after his own ideas. He disagreed with the other 23 scientist and went for himself to prove what he thought was necessary for you and I to know, the same as Yakub. This particular knowledge awakens you; you can't read [it] in no 6,000 year old history.

The true knowledge or science of the world that you and I are living in today was kept back, hidden and it was a secret among the scientist, until the world that you and I have known lived [out] its time and work that it was created to do. Today we are closing in or rather it's disappearing and a new world is budding or giving birth in place of an old one.

We the so-called American Negroes, [are] members, I repeat, from a Tribe of ours by the name of Shabazz. This man 50,000 years ago, remember that fifty thousand (50,000) years ago, not 6,000 years ago, fifty thousand (50,000). We, the Nation of Islam, the Nation of righteous, the Nation of peace, we have always experimented among ourselves or on this and that, and that's why we know we are the greatest and the wisest people in the universe because our study of the life on other planets; we don't find them experimenting among themselves or on their planet as we are; therefore, we know that we are the wisest people in the sun.

The so-called Negro, the black man, the lost and found member of a great original nation, the first on our planet: I want you to remember that we are the first on our planet. We are first before our planet. The planet didn't come after or rather before us we was before the planet. I want you to pay good attention, take notes on what I say, attack me on the truth of it if you want to, I don't have time to contend with you here this afternoon in this short time that I am given, but you can write me, you can attack me through mail if you want to, I will answer you....

Now, we, I say was before the earth; we could not claim ourselves as being the creators of the universe: The Sun, Moon and Star and the Earth, if we had been born or created after the earth, and if we came after the earth, then the earth is older than the God Who claimed to be master of the Earth. There is so much talk going on today, since Almighty God Allah has visited us and revealed to us the truth that is necessary, very much necessary, that I go into the past to bring you up with the truth to the present time, because that is the trouble with my people, they think they are inferior, they think they are something that God don't want himself. They think that their particular knowledge and way of life is like that of all of our people, regardless to what part of earth they live in, and some think that they are superior in wisdom, in education than any of their kind in the earth, this I say is a mistake that you are making yourself. It is due to the lack of knowledge of the black man. I want you to know these things before we go into argument over, “he is teaching hate; he’s teaching black supremacy.” I want to give to you the Blackmans’ history; you can say that he’s inferior, you can say that he’s not superior, you can say that he’s not the supreme people if you want to, that’s up to you, but I will give you his history and I defy you to disprove it.

“We don’t want religion.” Some of us are so proud. There are a lot of Atheist being born among the people. Today, living in a rich world and a fast world filled with sport and play, the so-called American Negro has been made drunken off such foolishness and today he’s proud to walk around some of them and say “I don’t believe in no God.” I want any Atheist to contend with me that he actually don’t believe in a God, and I can prove to you that you are mistaken; you do believe in a God, one that is Supreme over you;

we all have that. I say my beloved listeners, that if you feel that I am out of line, out of the order and law of the truth, you are welcome to attack me. But I would say before I go further, I thank you leaders of different organizations as I have learned that some of you are here, I thank you for your presence and I hope that you and I can agree on facts and live in unity together. And some of you religious people that do not actually confess Islam, but you are religious people of your choice, I am happy that you are here.

Christianity, Islam, and the Hindu religion, or Buddhism, is three of the greatest religions of the people today; Christianity is the youngest of them all. Buddhism is an old religion and Islam is as old as God Himself. Islam is not an organized religion, it's a religion to the very nature of God and of His people, it is the natural religion of God and His people, so says the Holy Qur'an 30:30. And how do we say that it's not if we are from the first Father or the Creator of the Universe; whatever His nature was, then we are that; if His nature was of evil, we are evil people, if His nature was good, then we are good people.

There is much confusion today over this revelation that has been revealed in America over the history of the two people, mainly black and white, that even I have lost a lot of friends amongst the Orthodox Muslims who are not able to agree that the nature in which we were created in is different from the nature of the white race, they are two different people altogether. I am so sorry for your lack of knowledge of self and others, but if we can listen and try to huddle over the truth that is said or being taught, you should bear me witness that I am after good for you, not evil, but for good. I am not after you to tie you in with your slave-master to make you one of the members of his family, as he has already destroyed us. About 85% or 95% per cent of us is destroyed by the slave master and his children according to one professor here today. Or, we don't have to do nothing but just glance at each other and we see and recognize the mark. You that want to further the destruction of your people, I want you to listen closely and after this, I hope you will bear witness to the truth that you would be a fool to destroy yourself.

CHAPTER 3

BLACKMAN AND ADAM

We, the original people of the Earth, the universe, have no birth record; there is no such thing as 6,000 years ago God created the heavens and the earth and we are all from Adam. Get away from that story. We the Black Nation of the Planet Earth, are not from Adam; it is the white race that is from Adam, but not you and I. He was the beginning or the father of this race of people 6,000 years ago. He was a god himself, the father of this race of people, his name was Yakub, they called him Jacob. He being a very smart and wise man with a large head, as you see that most of the white people have large heads. They used to call him the big head scientist in his day and time, because of the great massive head he had. I have to go after the history of you and I, to bring you up to our religion. We don't go and try to condemn without showing proof.

This particular nation of people, the black man, that my people have been made to despise, some of the college students, teachers and professors are even saying today that they don't even like black supremacy any more than they like white supremacy; they have not been able to remove white supremacy. They say now they don't like either one. I would like to question that professor on what kind of rule are you expecting to live under, or what color of people?

Since you have no knowledge of yourself and your history, and God Almighty has brought it to us, the best knower, that I am teaching to you today, I wish that you know this, that we were the supreme rulers for millions and billions of years. The white people that teach my people that I am teaching black supremacy only throws that in to make you dislike the truth that I'm teaching from God, and make you think that you are headed for trouble, as though they are not into white supremacy. They have been ruling us for 6,000 years and they think it's something of a crime that we say, that the Blackman is Supreme ruler.

CHAPTER 4

THE MAKING OF THE MOON

This, I want you to remember: that a long, long, long, long old time before the white man was ever thought of, we were ruling, not only this earth, but everything in the universe. We, our Fathers, are the makers and fashioners of the universe. Our Fathers made it. One of our Fathers, 66 trillion years ago, - don't think I'm making a mistake-66 trillion years ago, - pricking and blast this earth or planet that we're on, divided it, and used one part of it for a light to serve as a light on this part, to reflect the light of the sun at night: we call it Moon. That took place 66 trillion years ago, according to the teachings of Almighty God to me.

Just a moment, that is not the beginning of the Blackman, nor his creation or rule.

Six trillion years before that, we made the moon, to serve as a light to our earth, to take away Mars who had been serving as a moon to our earth before the making of the present moon, it was Mars. This Mars was so far away. Almighty God Allah said they prepared this present lifeless piece of our planet to reflect sunlight on our earth. It has a lot of affect on our earth, and on the vegetation, and on the lives of you and I. Some of the white people would like to go there and live, according to what I read.

I don't know why they want to go there, well I know why, but I don't know how they are going to live there, there is no life on that part of our planet, there's no water on it, unless it's somewhere in the heart of it, in a rock. And for 66 trillion years, she has been deprived of life, and water, vegetation, because after blasting away of that part of our earth, she lost all the water that was on that part, back on this part, after she was blast 12,000 miles away from the original pocket that we was in at that time.

This part dropped 36,000 miles, and found another pocket, and kept rotating, but the water we didn't loose, as we never lost water, water you cannot destroy, that's a good sign of the God. You cannot destroy the God, the Black nation with all of your planning, with all your science in murder or destruction of people, you cannot destroy all of us. You can destroy some of us, but not all of us.

CHAPTER 5

ATOMIC BOMBS TO FIGHT ALLAH

There're these scientists of this world, having ideas of trying to blow up these poison weapons, that if they are going, they want to carry us with them. It is their particular idea that they will do away with the earth with atomic weapon and hydrogen bombs, and I say you are mistaken, you won't be able to do that, because we have in our midst today a God that has the power over your thinking. He has power over what you do; you have it in your Bible, he created this mist that's suppose to go and brings out a weapon, listen, this is a warning to the enemy, and to the believer, that if I have power over his mist, I have power over his weapons; I have power over his thinking, and that he will learn through attacking me through my people, that he won't be able to win in a war with me.

With the civilized people of the earth today, doing everything to destroy themselves, it is time that my people here know the truth and know how strong their nation is, and know how strong the God of the nation. The reason that you're trembling, fear in the face of white people, it is because of the lack of knowledge of yourself and the God of you and I, and the god that created the white man, and that people, and the limited knowledge that they have which is number six (6). You have no right to fear white people today; to accept the truth, we are the winners; we are the victorious people; we will rule.

CHAPTER 6

ORIGIN OF THE WHITE RACE - DEVILS

We have been here a long, long, time. It was a black man by the name of Yakub, 6,600 years ago who grafted the white race out of us. They are from us. They have tried to cover their birth and their father and their mother by saying that they came from sea life; then, if they came from sea life, then sea life is their god, or their father; or that they're from animals. They would rather say that most anything is their god, other than to say a black man was their god. Thcy don't likc you and I, because of the very nature of which they were created.

We can't look for brotherly love from a man that was made to be the enemy of you. You can't look for it, don't expect it. I am not angry with the white race because they hate me, they was made to hate me. We can't get away from that in which by nature we are.

So we have here six days in the Bible that God created the heaven and the earth, we have six periods in the Holy Qur'an, and other periods that is divided into six, that God created the heavens and the earth, but what you have in the Bible there, dated back to 6,000 years ago, means this: That it had taken their father, Yakub, 600 years to make a race out of another race. He was grafting out of darkness, or out of the Blackman for 600 years, to bring out a complete white man altogether different by nature than that in which he was taken from.

These are facts that I defy your colleges or university professors to dispute. There are so many of you whispering, going around saying, "This old story, we all are from God; we are all brothers; we all are alike." I say to you my people, stop telling other than the truth, you are not like white people. You can't deceive God, nor can you deceive anyone whom God have opened

His heart for understanding. You want them to think that you are in so much love with them because you have been made like that by them. You fear them because their fathers put fear in your fathers when they was babies. And now that you have nursed from your grandparents breast which has come down into the breast of the present mothers of the black people here, and every child that they birth has a trembling fear of white people. I say to you my friends, this will get you hell. What I would like that you do: come to Allah and accept Islam and that fear will be removed. You will not have any fear. You fear because you have no knowledge of that which you fear.

Again I say to you, that these religions that are burning out or being born, so numerous for the last 6,000 years, it is due to the fact that Almighty God Allah did not try to teach or further His religion after the birth of the white race, because He had agreed to let the white race rule according to his own wishes. They created them to try them at ruling. As you would find it in the Qur'an and you will find it in the Bible where that Adam was given authority over everything to rule it, that was the white race, bringing into subjection everything of life, even the fish of the sea, birds, animals, everything, all men other than their own race, they have accomplished that. And you have to give them credit, that they have done everything that the book said they would do.

They have forced the black man to bow and submit to their rule for the past 6,000 years, and they have trained and made wild animals, birds, sea life to submit to their rule, everything has submitted to them, but the God of heaven and a circle of scientists that they could never get into that circle, which is left to start a new world for the Blackman. I hope that you won't think hard of me for digging into these roots, but it takes these roots, pulled up out of the dark to show you yourself. You have heard probably that the truth shall be told, though I have read too the consequences of telling the truth in the last days; we're suffering that consequence, because 20 million blind, deaf and dumb, people here, spiritually blind, deaf, and dumb, is worth the life of myself and even a portion of my followers to bring in to the life of truth, but nevertheless the Jesus did not tell you what that truth was, that would make you free, you don't have it there, no. He could not tell you at that time, he was 2,000 years ahead of the time when the truth should be told.

We're most hated because we have the knowledge of such truth. No man that is in power wants to be taken out of power and authority, and be replaced by another, no. But it is time. I think that God has blessed the whiteman greatly. I think the white race should be willing if God would tell them to stick up their hands and let's go now. I think they should be willing to go.

In America where that they came, killed off the original settlers here, the Red Indians, who were exiled out of what is know as East India today, 16,000 years ago, that was 10,000 years before there was a Caucasian on our planet. They came through the Baring Straits over that ice and started making a home here in the Western Hemisphere. At that time the Lord God, Almighty Allah said, they referred to this part of the planet as a prisoner island, because of this people, the Indians, Red Indians. They were disobedient to Allah, and to the law of God, and refused to accept Islam. Islam has always been the teaching or the religion of God, but not always under that name, but the meaning or principle of belief and practice has always been the same: We believe in one God. We submit to that God, entire submission to His will is Islam, that's what we call Islam. And that has always been among us.

We never disobey Allah until Yakub made a disobedient race of people who would become and did become the very enemy of Almighty God Allah, and his people. Then they began to take us away, stripped us away into their evil disobedience and today now they have all but 90 per cent of the people of the blind population, I should say, disobeying God Almighty following after their own evil ways and other gods they have set up besides Him claiming or giving that god which did not create anything, and who has not the power to guide or the power of mercy and love for those who would follow - giving them the glory and honor that they should give to Allah. I say my friend, this may be stinging, but it's facts. As I don't get out to teach very often, but on such occasion as this wherein that I can speak to a thousand, ten thousand of you, I would like to speak with you and give to you the truth.

The Original Man, the first and the last: Go to Asia. Go to Africa. You don't find nobody running around there unless he's a Christian missionary, preaching the end of the world. They don't have that particular nature to say that such and such a time, that we black people here in Africa and in Asia will be destroyed by God. No, it is Europe, it is America, it is the Christian people who preaches the end of the world. It is those people whom the end has been set. Their time was limit to live on our planet earth when they were created. It is the white race, that have a certain time to live, and that is 6,000 years. And the black people have no beginning on our planet, if it is, why? We don't have a birth record of it. And they have no ending. As I say, you can't destroy us all, because we always have one among us who is waiting for you to just [attempt] evil acts to destroy us, and that will be the end of you.

CHAPTER 7

THE JUDGEMENT OF THIS WORLD

The Judgement of the world is so close, I'm forced to tell you what I am telling you. The Black man of America is so dumb and so helpless, that he is a prey in the hands of the white people. He's easy to forget his own hurt. The white man can kill all of his family today, and tomorrow you will shake hands with him. That's right. He has been made an absolute living coward. He's so humble and submissive, and so dumb and ignorant, that the whiteman can use him for anything he wants. They want the whiteman's friendship, and they have been working on it for four hundred years, and they're just as far off from it today, as they were four hundred years ago. Look in Mississippi today. Look in Philadelphia, look in Chicago, look in New York City. Look in all the cities of America, and you will find your brother's head bleeding with knots on it, from police brutality, and from any whiteman who wants to beat him up. Due to the fact that he's humble, he's scared to death, he won't put up a fight to protect himself, and the whiteman is like the wolf. He don't care whether the lamb submit or not. And he don't care whether the man likes it or the lamb likes it, he eats him just the same.

Now today under this hypocritical integration, the white man desires to deceive the negro further; pretending that he is his friend, pretending that he wants him now to enter our society, be a member of us, why, because he hears Allah's name being mentioned a lot. They don't want you to come to Allah, they don't want you to believe in Islam. They are against Islam, they are against Allah, they never did teach your parents and my parents nothing of Allah nor of Islam. They didn't teach our parents their own religion. Three hundred years, our parents was under the lash and burden of slavery, that they was deprived of any knowledge of God, or scripture of any kind. They deprived our fathers of reading and writing, which is the art or science that is used to conveying our ideas to others, you were deprived of.

Less than a hundred years ago he permitted you to go to his church or rather in a church to yourself. And you have been segregated from them every since. Now today, he says,"let us take him in our society" for what? What do you want to do with him? He don't look like you. We're watching you; we know what you want to do with him. You want to take him to hell with you that's all. I say that's to bring you out the real raw truth, the white race was not created for the hereafter. They were created for hell, and hell for them. You have it in both Bible and Qur'an, that's why that there world is coming to an end, and that's why God tells you that He will make manifest the man of sin in that day and time, at the end of their world. And you would be told then the truth of this people. That they were not created to be the people of God, of truth and justice, they are created to be the enemies of God, of truth and justice, and of those who believe in a God of truth and justice.

CHAPTER 8

JESUS: ONLY A PROPHET

We the Muslims here in your midst, we believe in Freedom, Justice and Equality, the truth of God, and the truth of His prophets, and the Scriptures in which God gave to those prophets. We believe in it. We believe in Jesus, we believe in Abraham, we believe in Moses, and the scriptures in which they brought to us, the people. We don't believe Jesus is anymore a son of God than you or I, who are the people of God or the Righteous. This is a scandal that they have made you to believe, which is absolutely other than the truth, that some spooky something went around Mary, talked to her, and after that spook left her, she was pregnant.

This is the base of the Christian belief, that there was a miraculous life and death of Jesus. I say my beloved black people here this afternoon, cut that out, that is all false, Joseph was the father of Jesus.

No spook makes flesh and blood. Jesus was flesh and blood and his mother bared him in pain, and he had to go nine months before he was born like any other normal child, and he died the death of any other man. You say but he rose from the dead. That is something that you don't understand. If he has rose from the dead, and became a man again, then why haven't you and I seen him? For 2,000 years we haven't met up with that man. You say he's gone to heaven, what kind of heaven, he didn't change from nothing but the earth, and if he's going back to heaven, he went back to the earth. He didn't come from no other planet, there is no other planet that you and I can live on, or be born on, if we were born on the earth. We can't go to no other planet and live, that's foolishness to talk such; we did not come from there, and were not returning to such, and there is no such thing as a Jesus and a God standing on any other planet looking at you and I.

The God is here on this earth. This is the God where you and I live. This is the heaven, this is the hell. Hell and heaven is not a certain place, or a particular place, it is the condition of our lives. You won't be able to come through no tombstone, or even through the dust, because they don't come back after they go there. We have had life, they last for trillions of years and never have anybody returned from that earth that went back to it. When you go back to the earth, you don't rise anymore.

You say, oh yes I believe it. Ok, let's pick a simple example: There was a ship [that] sunk at sea, a submarine blasted it, and all the soldiers went down in the sea. Alright. Didn't nobody go down there and pick them up and bury them did they? They had died right? Ok, The fish ate them or some other sea animals. And maybe you caught one of the fish that ate some of these soldiers. And you ate the fish, and now when the trumpet is blown where is that soldier coming from? Your limited knowledge of science makes you destroy yourself or cause much harm to come to you.

You say alright, you're on land, well alright then, suppose a wild animal ate one of you out here on land ok, he finally dies and his carcass go and then enrich the earth, and fertilizes green grass, a cow or a sheep or something come and eat that grass. Then you kill that animal and eat him, where will they then find that man? Don't you wish for no resurrection of no dead because you have ate many dead yourself.

CHAPTER 9

THE RESURRECTION AND THE HEREAFTER

The resurrection of the dead only means bringing up people, mentally dead or blind, deaf, and dumb as they call it. Blind means that you are too spiritually blind that you cannot understand or see the truth and distinguish it from falsehood. And deaf means your ears are so rebellious against truth, that you will not allow them to listen to the truth. And your tongue, or you're dumb because that you don't allow your tongue to practice the truth and nor receive the teachings of the truth, therefore your tongue is like one that cannot even speak, because it knows nothing about the truth nor can it talk on the truth. So you're called blind, deaf, and dumb. And there is no such thing as the physical body coming up out of the earth, nor the physical form will take on a new voice, you'll have a new body, from this old one, but it is like this according to the teachings of the Qur'an, that it will be reversed instead of going into decay, it will go into use again, like an old tree that starts budding out new blossoms, or new limbs, this is what will happen to you that see the hereafter. You will start growing into a new growth, which will take you back to your youth again, into teenagers, and you will remain like that if you live here a thousand years, because there won't be any decaying on the other side, what I mean the other side after the destruction or disappearance of the whitemans' world, there will be no decay in the blackman. Everything under this number six decays, because it was built upon that particular principle or nature, that it should decay and die away.

I say again to you now the religion, all kinds of religions have been practiced. You say I don't want your Islam, I don't want your Allah. What do you know about Allah, and what do you know about Islam? Do you mean to tell me that you are so great, you are so powerful, you are so wise, that you will not bow to any other superior being other than yourself? When that you are living under the authority of a Supreme being over you. We only say to you to submit to the will of the Divine Supreme Being, One Who is wiser than we all, One more powerful than we all, One Who is hearing and knowing, Who is capable of reversing the whole of the creation, and reproducing it, and One Who is able to pass it out of existence and bring in a new one altogether. You would not bow and submit to a man that has the power to take you out of the earth, bring you into a living being, and have the power to remove you from the planet.

Did I say to you that you are rebellious? Yes you are. You don't take time to learn; you are to proud; you are resisting God, because you have never been taught Allah and Islam by the whiteman. It is against the nature of white people to believe in Allah. They can if they want to. We have a few white people that is in Islam, brought up in it, just like you have been brought up in the white man's Christianity. Christianity is a religion that the whiteman preaches. It is a religion that was organized.

It is not the religion that came with God and the Prophets; it's a religion that they organized. And they organized it to their own satisfaction. And they certainly have been successful under it, but you and I have not. Why? Why have not you been successful in Christianity? It is because you did not know the tricks that was in it. You took the wrong end of it.

You're not successful in trying to play the whiteman's game of civilization; you're both two different people altogether. You cannot be successful in trying to integrate in white people, because they will destroy you. You won't destroy them, but they will destroy you. Some of you are so dumb, that you would like to be destroyed. But I say to you that the Black man is not what you think he is; you're looking at the one that has been corrupt, one that has been marred, destroyed. But I say, the real one, that you are from, you don't know him so well. We are this original people, and we are from the originator of the heavens and the earth, when and where it took place. We are from that particular Father. And I say again and again, we are not equal, we are not born of the same father and mother, we are not the same people by nature the same.

CHAPTER 10

CURSE OF YAKUB'S CIVILIZATION

The white race are a weaker physical people than the original black people. They came from the original black people, and through the grafting; they were made weaker. And by being made physically weaker, they were taught wickedness by their father; they weren't taught to do good; he taught them to be evil; he taught them how to murder and lie when they were even in the mother's womb; he practiced on the nurse: told the nurse how to tell the mother lies. And the lie went down into her baby. And the baby, when it comes here, is born with that lie, and knows by nature how to lie and deceive others. That's why you have it in 8:32 of John, that the Jesus says "I know your father, he was a murderer and a liar from the beginning". This means Yakub, Yakub's idea was to make a people to be the ruler of our people, or the people that they are from. And he taught his people to murder the black people, destroy them, and build up your own people on the earth; this, the white man has followed to both letter and the spirit.

At that time when they were grafted out of our people, the population of our planet earth according to the teachings of Almighty God to me was fifty-hundred-million people on our Planet. Five billion people was the population when Yakub began grafting the white race. And the white race has caused that fifty or five billion people to come to this number today: forty four hundred million. They have destroyed six hundred million of our people since they have been on the planet, and they are still destroying them. They were made like that, you can't blame them, you have to blame yourself. Their father was the one that made these people murderers. When they can't murder a bird or can't murder some harmless animal or murder some harmless so called negro, they murder

can't stay there unless you carry enough of this atmosphere to live on. You've got to distill all your food from the earth to eat. And even if you was on Mars or Venus, you couldn't eat the food there. Every Planet carries its own weight of life or its own kind of life, and you and I cannot just adapt our lives with that life on that planet. You can't drink the water on that planet it will kill you. You have to confine your own life to this earth where you came from. And I don't care where you go, you will finally return to this earth, if you have to drift back to space, you'll come back to the earth.

You must know today the time is at hand, and I must tell you, it is my people that I'm after. They are the ones that are dead. They are the dead of the Bible. The whiteman is all wise to all that I'm saying. I'm not trying to tcach him, he knows. It is you that don't know. I'm not trying to force you to follow me. I'm only trying to tell you the truth, you follow whom you please. Allah can do without you. We have oceans of people on this planet, and if you never join on to them, they will never miss you.

CHAPTER 11

THE SLAVE, MASTER AND HIS RELIGION

Christianity versus Islam: Christianity as I said, and you can bear me witness, is an organized religion, it is not a religion that Jesus is the author or founder of. Jesus knew nothing of Christianity in the day he was living, Christianity came after his death. Jesus was of the same religion that I am teaching to you today, Islam. Jesus was a Muslim. He said that he came not to destroy the law of the prophets. Then they makes sense over here where he says in the older times; he said, "an eye for an eye, a tooth for a tooth," meaning, Moses' law taught them that. And for you now, if he smacks you on one side of the cheek, turn the other, knock out your tooth go ahead and give him another tooth to knock out. This was the slave-master's way of making some harmless slaves. He didn't want the slave to strike back, so he tell them that the book say this: "You shall not throw railing for railing." They even tell me now, "Why do you teach them to hate us?" They never say why I'm teaching to hate that they call hate. Then you are wrong. You shouldn't do that if the whiteman have did that, then you should not do that yourself, you should bring about love among us. But I say that all the while I am teaching you, they are giving hell right on.

They can't do any better; their nature don't teach them to love you and treat you like they treat themselves. And you being an original Black person, you yourselves cannot by nature, be one of them by no means, unless that you are made into them. Again, I say you are a fool to want to go and be just like your slave master; you are a fool to want to destroy your identity, you are a fool to want to be equal members in their society, when you are not. You cannot demand the slave master to give you equal recognition, when you are not; he's the master and you are the slave, you can't do that. You cannot demand him to give you fair employment; that's his job, he made it, and he do what he please with it. He will take his own people if he wants them in front of you, and any other nation will do the same. What you and I should do is go make a job for our own people, and for ourselves.

But we are a bit lazy. We don't want to work and produce work for our people. We want to beg other people. I say you are well educated to a certain extent. You can with your educators produce employment for your own people if you would unite, and get to yourself to do it. You cannot with 20 million people here, dependent on the white race, white America, to produce or created jobs for you and build your needs, build houses, farm for you, everything that you want, from a pair of socks, to a hat on your head he has to produce. I say this thing is not going to last forever, even if they wanted to do so, it won't last forever. They are now a great people in population, and you are like your fathers was in servitude slavery, begging your masters for bread, begging master for clothes, begging master for a shovel. If you are turned down, you should not think hard of them, think hard of yourself. For one hundred years, they have said that we are free, though I know, you know, that you are not freed in deed, but I say, they said that we are free, lets try and exercise some of it. Go to the master and say "Let me go from you, help me to go from you, and help me to stay from you." A lazy man don't ever want to go out from a house that he can get away with or get along without work. Most of our leaders don't want to go to work or put their people to work to build a nation, because of the temptation of the white man's world. He says, "I'm just as much a citizen as you. I am entitled to this." That's a coward talking to the father. We know that we are not equal in sharing America; why should we boast that we are. We know we are not citizens. We could not be citizens unless we were white people.

CHAPTER 12

SEPARATION, NOT INTEGRATION

We are alien. We were brought here, not to be made citizens of this country, equal citizens with the white man, nor to receive equal justice. We were brought here for burden bearers. And you are fighting them today to try and force them against their own will, and against the very law of nature, to accept you as their equal, and share with you equally in all they have. This is against the very law of nature, they can't do that. And you would like to destroy yourself into yourself, by marrying into them, and they are not going to let you do that. There is no intelligent decent white people who wants a negro as his son-in-law, or daughter-in-law. And there is no decent and intelligent black man who wants a white son-in-law nor a white daughter-in-law.

Being ignorant of yourself, and like many other African people that the white man has destroyed by going into them, destroying their identity as he have you, he had a better chance at you because you was in his house. As I say, 85 per cent, as it is said by certain writers, 95 per cent of us is destroyed by the white man's blood. You thinking that you are going to get up to his equal by opening your doors to admitting him in, you're only destroying yourself; he's wise, he don't intend on destroying his people, not with your blood. The White Camellia, and the National Party in America, the Ku Klux Klan, I don't blame them for wanting to keep you out of their family. I don't blame them for not wanting the integration law to pass, because they know what will be the results. I don't want it myself. No. I want separation.

Being eaten and destroyed by a people, and then I should say to them: that they teach me for the purpose of destroying me?

No. I want to leave you. We can't get along in peace. We have given you an example in Los Angeles of the white man's very nature. We tried to be at peace with them, we go unarmed, and they don't like that. They pounce upon us like wild animals out of the jungle, and start shooting us up even in our Temple. Killing one, and wounding five or six others, one or two permanently. They want to take care of you in their hospitals with a bullet through your body, or a vast artery, or the spine, they would rather take care of you there cripple, make mock of you to have you remorse, and they say, "there's a nigger I shot", there's a nigger I killed, there's a nigger I beat."

I say to you and I, as Moses said to the Hebrews, under Pharaoh, up, let us get out of here. With the whiteman's anger in the south and his hatred of his once slave, that he don't want him even to sit on the seat besides him. How can you expect that red sun burnt white man with one side of his mouth turning his mouth dyed with brown mule tobacco, to be so friendly with you, to take you today as a brother. The Federal Government has to send an Army to permit one even to get into his school, I say to you my Brother Meredith you was a fool. I say to the government, if you have to sent an army to put me in this school, and to watch me to keep him from killing me, what will he do after you leave? They're called ignorant. No intelligent person would take such foolish chance. I go to your door and knock on it and you tell me "No, don't come in my house". I say to you, thank you, I will go away. I will not go out and tell the police, "Make him let me in his housc, I'm suppose to go in there." NO. I would be ashamed to tell the police that. Some of our people, lying down on their restaurant floors, and coffee shops, begging and praying, "Let me have a cup of coffee in here with you, let me have a sandwich in here with you, let me have a meal with you." I'm ashamed of my own people, for being so ignorant. The intelligent way to get a person to respect you, is to first respect yourself, and others.

CHAPTER 13

. . . AND THIS IS CHRISTIANITY?

Islam, the natural religion of man, is the only cure for the so-called American Negro. It put a sense of dignity in that man; for the first time you feel like a man; for the first time you feel like you should not beg other people to do that for you that you can do for yourself. And for the first time in your life, that you find love in your heart for yourself and your kind. You love your people after Islam. But Christianity divides you. We are the results or victims of Christianity. Who made us spiritually blind? It was white Christians who went after our people and put them in chains 400 years and brought them here.

Some of us say that Christianity is God's religion and it's Jesus' religion. So foolish a thing. Christian beliefs are based on three (3) gods, is based on life after death, based on Jesus rising from the dead, and had a miraculous birth and death. This you have to believe before you could ever be called a Christian, or believer in Christianity. This is contrary from the God's own nature, I am thy God, and me and me alone should you serve. I know no other God. I am the first, and I am the last. It is written, in the birthright. Alright then, how can you say that he is the god, His son is the god and His holy ghost is the god? How can you say something like that?

There is no such thing as Jesus was the equal with God. How could he could be equal with his own maker? He admitted that he was not equal with his Father. He admitted that he had no power, but that which he would be given or was given to him from His Father. He said I am not His equal, no. I am from Him. I am His servant. Think over that. And I know nothing, only what He has given to me, and I can do nothing without Him. Here you come saying he is the equal, he was in the day, and all the like of that, when the God was present. Was Jesus here when the heaven and the earth was created? No. He was from that Father, but he was not the equal in making the universe with his Father. The universe was here when he was born, like us. And he knew not how to build a universe, but my Fathers built one. And my wisdom and understanding has not went that high yet to understand how to take my will, and put it into space, and start a planet to swirling out there in a pocket, and create life on it. No, I can't do that, but my Fathers did that. And Jesus did not do that.

Jesus was no more than Abraham or Moses, he was just a prophet. He did his work and he prophesied that I go away; meaning, He will die like all other prophets. "But nevertheless, the Father will send you one to bring you into the knowledge of truth. I can't tell it all myself, but he will send you one. He said you should understand."

The white race has made them a little religion to catch black people with. Christianity, if you study it, you will find that the whole of its teachings is nothing but slavery. It's to enslave black people for the service of white people; that's all it's for. Attack me on any of it, and I will prove to you I will lay your religion so bare, barer than your feet, to show you that it's nothing but slavery teachings. There is no such thing as Jesus sitting in a heaven waiting for the final Judgement, he won't be here when the final judgement come anymore than Moses or Abraham. He's gone back to the earth, or rather he's embalmed, and he will stay there another well 8,000 years. They embalmed him to last 10,000 years, and that his body will disappear at the end of ten thousand years. And it will disappear at this very hour if air is let in that tube that he's in. He's not alive, he looks just like he did the day that they killed him, but he's not alive. Go there and yell to him all you want to, he can't speak, he can't hear you either.

I visited in 59, the tomb Abraham, his wife Sarah, and this other woman Hagar, they have them over there. I also saw Jacob's tomb, there over there. But let me tell you one thing, you have been made to believe everything that you hear, without even trying to study it and examine it to see whether or not it was the truth. Just so as long as the devil say "here it is nigger," you took it for granted that it was the truth.

We have the emblem of Christianity as a cross, and a crucified man on it right? That is the emblem of Christianity, which means that the people who follow this religion will suffer persecution, they will suffer enslavement, they will suffer death under this particular religion, they will be bound in the power of the white man hand and feet. They won't be able to move their hands for their use, they won't be able to use their feet to walk to that in which that they want to. Their steps will be limited. They are nailed to the cross of Christianity under the power of the white man. Their heads is crowned with thorns, not literally thorns, but that particular ignorant knowledge of the truth, going through their brain cells, like a literal thorn being pricked into the brain. There you are, unable to think for self. Christianity deprives you of that. That's the thorns in your head now. You are stabbed through the heart, you are unable to feel the wounds, you died with grief and sorrow under Christianity. Islam is different. The Holy

Qur'an says "He that believe in Allah, and in His prophets, and in His book, keeps up prayer, pays the poor rate, there is no fear for him nor shall he grieve". And that is right. As soon as you believe in Christianity, it increases your fear.

CHAPTER 14

THE CRESCENT AND THE CROSS

So I say to you my beloved brothers and sisters, the time is running on, but I must take a look at this first: If Christianity is the right religion, why must you use a murder sign? That ole cross on yonder field, an emblem, the Christians say of sinning or something like that. Someday, the Christians say, I hope you exchange this cross; for what, for a starry crown. I also say that with them, I hope someday you will change that old cross, to a starry crown. We, the Muslim people, hate the death sign.

We, the Muslim people, worship God in the best manner. We take for our sign for a religion, the Sun, the Moon, and the Star. They call it the Crescent, the background is the red, it means the Sun. It means this physically, that the Sun gives the freedom of light and warmth. The Moon or Star rather, is a sign or emblem of Justice. In the physical world, it serves as a guiding thing for us in the night, and also the Moon she's in our flag, or in our representing our religion, as equality. In the physical world she helps the Sun to feed the vegetation at night while the Sun doesn't shine on it. She helps the Sun keeps life in equal balance at her equator. This is the magnetic power of the Moon on the Earth, and we call her a sign of equality, because she came from the earth, and now she's helping the earth and confined to the power of the live earth, which she was once of, and is unable to pull away from it, because she don't have the life to leave, now, no conscious, to leave, or to pull her away from there. This is a sign for you and I and the wisdom that you and I should learn. You are a mentally dead nation here, in the midst of a live nation, as the Holy Qur'an say, "Allah will bring the dead from the living, and the living from the dead". You are a dead nation and a live nation. Now you can't leave this people until life has been infused in yourself. While you are dead, you are rotating around this people, and can't get away from them. This teaching is to give you life, so that you might find a sphere of your own that you can rotate in.

So therefore we have a sign of our religion as the Crescent, I say you don't like it. Do you not like the Sun, do you not like the moon, do you not like the stars, yes you like all of that because that's essential for your own well being or your own life. But without the Sun you couldn't live. And without the Moon's work that she's doing for the earth, her title waves would soon sweep us off into dry land; they have no control over them if it was left loose. But the moon keeps the title waves reaching up at her; therefore, they are commanded that they shall not set over the bound or the bound is set in the ocean. And also the stars.

We are asking America for freedom in deed. We are asking America for equal justice under her law of justice. We are asking America to let us build ourselves up as equal human beings as she has; build ourselves up in the world of nations as equal to the nations. We must remember my friends, that we have to go from scratch to get to that which is something, that which is salvation to you and I. Don't look for integration, look for separation.

You can never be successful in trying to live in the house with the white man as a member of his family, unless you're going to be his slave, and you and your fathers lived in his house for 300 years as his slave and now in a hundred years, you are still in the status of a free-slave. You have nothing. You have helped him fight his wars, you have helped him till the soil of America. You have helped him to build a great civilization that is absolutely not equal by any of his brothers. He's the richest of all his brothers, and he has the greatest country of all of his brothers. And you and I have helped them, and our fathers before us for 400 years to come into this great richness that he's enjoying. He has shot his own brothers down that he said was an enemy to us, to him. And then he has put us on our own brothers to kill our own brothers, and we did that [because] he said [our brother] was an enemy of his. Now today I say, try to study for yourself, do you see any hope, do you see any future for 20 million so-called American Negroes in America for yourself, living as you are living, seeking jobs, employment that is created by the whiteman. Do you see a future for yourself, and your nation for the duration of your nation's life? Not under the same condition or in the same condition, begging the white man to go and create jobs for you to be hired on and pay out of his own pocket.

The Black man in America faces a serious economic problem today and the white race's Christianity cannot solve it. You, the so-called American Negro, with the help of Allah can solve your own problem. The truth must be recognized by the black man. He, himself, has assisted greatly in creating this serious problem of unemployment, insecurity and lack. Before the black man can begin to gain economic security, he must be awakened from the dead and gain knowledge, understanding and wisdom which will enable him to follow my teachings. Islam and only Islam will point the way out of the entanglement of "want in the midst of plenty" for the followers of Islam, the true religion of the black nation.

Closing Note

PERSECUTION FOLLOWS THE COMING OF GOD

He (Mr. W.F. Muhammad, God in person) chose to suffer 3 1/2 years to show His love for His people, who have suffered over 300 years at the hands of a people who by nature are evil and wicked and have no good in them. He was persecuted, sent to jail in 1932, and ordered out of Detroit, on May 26, 1933. He came to Chicago in the same year and was arrested almost immediately on His arrival and placed behind bars.

He submitted Himself with all humbleness to his persecutors. Each time he was arrested, he sent for me so that I might see and learn the price of Truth for us, the so-called American Negroes (members of the Asiatic nation).

He was well able to save Himself from such suffering, but how else was the scripture to be fulfilled? We followed in His footsteps, suffering the same persecution.

My people are yet sound asleep to the knowledge of the good that is being carried on for their deliverance. The whole world of our kind awaits the awakening, and our awakening is the last step in the Resurrection and Judgment of the world. It is a sin that we were put so soundly to sleep. The end of the world has arrived, and most of us know it not. Our enemies' greatest desire is that we remain asleep. My people fight and oppose the God of our own salvation.

Allah chose for us Islam as a religion. He desires to set us in Heaven at once, on condition that we submit to Him and accept the religion of Islam, the religion of God and His prophets. In the religion (Islam), He offers us universal friendship, and we who have submitted to Him know this to be true.

We know white people have and will continue to persecute anyone who offers help to us, the so-called American Negroes (Asiatics). Should persecution or even death stop the worthy help that will save the lives of the so-called Negroes? No, it shall not.

The so-called Negroes are absolutely friendless and have sought in vain friendship from their enemies, due to the ignorance of self and their enemies. Now they are offered universal friendship if they will only accept their own (Allah and Islam).

Seek first the friendship of your own people and then the friendship of other (if there is any friendship in the others).

We have made the grave mistake of Lazarus and the Prodigal Son, (St. Luke: Chapter 15), the one who was so charmed over the wealth and food of the rich man that he could not leave his gate to seek the same for himself, - regardless of the disgraceful condition in which the rich man puts him, even to sending his dogs to attack him. The angels had to come and take him away.

The other (Prodigal Son), being tempted by the loose life of strange women, drinking, gambling, and adultery, caused him to love the stranger's way of life so much so that it cost him all that he originally possessed (self-independence and Divine Guidance). His Father (God in person) had to come and be his representative to again meet his brothers, family, and friends.

Nothing fits the description of us better, the so-called Negroes (Asiatics). Many of us today are so lazy that we are willing to suffer anything rather than go for self. It is true that our God has come to set us in Heaven, but not a Heaven wherein we will not have to work.

Fear is the worst enemy that we have, but entire submission to Allah (God) and His Messenger will remove this fear. The white race put fear in our foreparents when they were babies, so says the word of Allah.

We must have for our peace and happiness (the 17,000,000 so-called Negroes) that which other nations have.

This beforementioned peace and happiness cannot come under any other flag but our own. If God desires for us such joy, why shouldn't we give up begging and be real men and sit with the rulers of the earth, ruling our own?

Our first step is to give back to the white man his religion (Christianity), his church, and his names. These three are chains of slavery that hold us in bondage to them. We are free when we give up the above three.

The so-called Negroes must know that they have been deceived and must be brought face to face with God and the devil. They must get away from the old slavery teaching that Jesus, who was killed 2,000 years ago, is still alive somewhere waiting and listening to their prayers.

He was only a prophet like Moses and the other prophets and had the same religion (Islam). He did His work and is dead like others of His time and has no knowledge of their prayers to Him.

Since Islam over-ran mankind in the seventh century after Jesus and is still a power over man, why did not the translators of the Bible mention it? Why didn't they give us the name of the religions of the prophets, since they claim a religion for Jesus?

Subscribe!

To The Fastest Growing Newspaper Available, Which Gives It Straight, Regardless of Whom Or What!

(see membership info.)

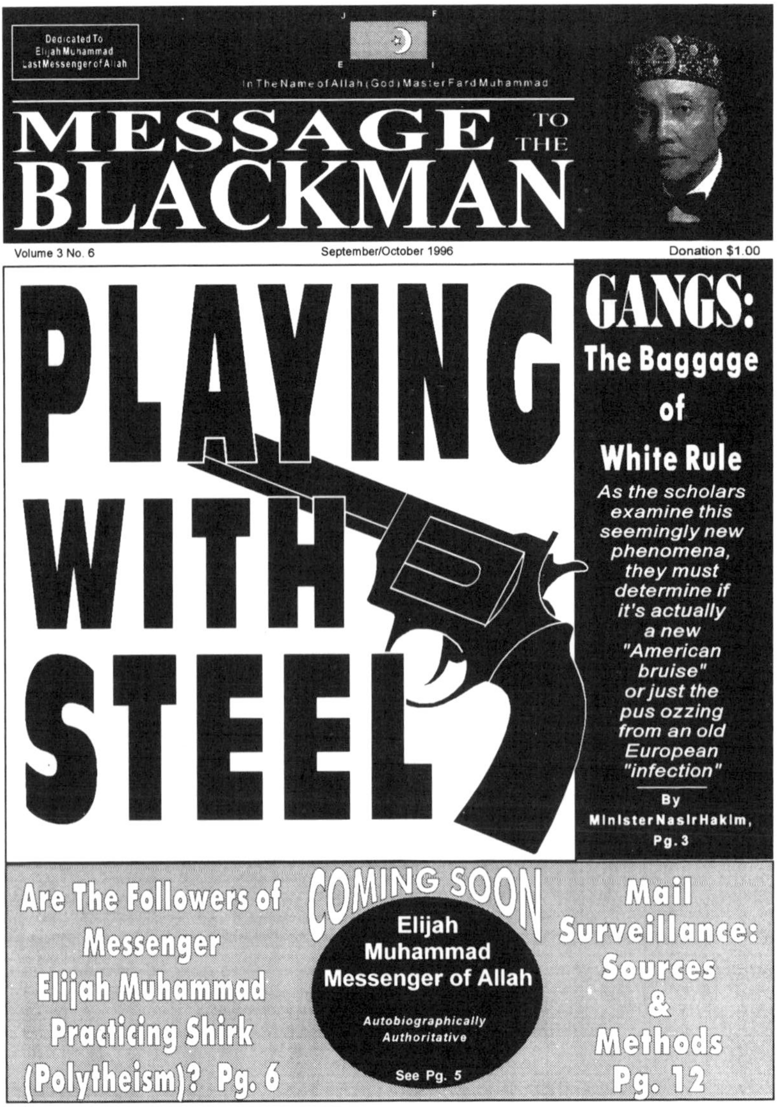

Dedicated To Elijah Muhammad Last Messenger of Allah

J F E I

In The Name of Allah (God) Master Fard Muhammad

MESSAGE TO THE BLACKMAN

Volume 3 No. 6 | September/October 1996 | Donation $1.00

PLAYING WITH STEEL

GANGS: The Baggage of White Rule

As the scholars examine this seemingly new phenomena, they must determine if it's actually a new "American bruise" or just the pus ozzing from an old European "infection"

By Minister Nasir Hakim, Pg. 3

Are The Followers of Messenger Elijah Muhammad Practicing Shirk (Polytheism)? Pg. 6

COMING SOON

Elijah Muhammad Messenger of Allah

Autobiographically Authoritative

See Pg. 5

Mail Surveillance: Sources & Methods Pg. 12

Messenger Elijah Muhammad Propagation Society

(MEMPS) Humbly Invites You To Become A Valued Member!

The **MEMPS MEMBERSHIP** is an effective cost cutting way to invest in various forms of Messenger Elijah Muhammad's works.

These works consist of an extensive amount of lectures, public meetings, national and international interviews, radio and television broadcasts, annual conventions, temple dedications, and various table talks.

Much of these works were not available to the public at the time they were produced. Additionally, with the limited forms of media at that time, reproduction of these works were not as easy as it is today. Most of these works were lifted or transferred from reel to reel recorder and much of the video footage was originally on 35mm film, which was very common and accessible in those days. The public did not have nearly as many reel to reel recorders and 35mm film projectors as they now have of audio cassette players and Video Cassette Recorders (VCR's).

The same could stand as a reason why many who actually was in the Nation of Islam, didn't know much of this information from the Messenger existed; consequently, they have come to see that even they may still need clarity on various points and positions Elijah Muhammad, Messenger of Allah taught about.

Our objective is to deliver these truths of the Messenger to as many of our people who seeks it. Regardless of their respective understanding of the teachings and the ways they are expressing them, a membership, which makes these great works easy to get at a very low cost, was highly necessary. We are confident that those who seek these words of the Messenger will greatly benefit.

We have the largest accessible collection of Messenger Elijah Muhammad's works in the world!

Not only is our collection in hard copy, but we have, to date, the ONLY computerized database of Elijah Muhammad's teachings in the world!

Our publications of Elijah Muhammad are drawn from hundreds of lectures, articles, video & audio tapes which makes them highly comprehensive and unmatched since Muhammad's Temple No. 2 publishing.

Our database will be online (Fax) soon along with the availability of the 1st encyclopedic anthology of his works!

Benefits:

✦ **FREE 1 YEAR SUBCRIPTION TO MESSAGE TO THE BLACKMAN**
Message To The Blackman is a hard hitting tabloid that deals with many of different perspectives of issues for and about Black people. Our "slant" is that of critical analysis. Many have chosen themselves as leaders of our people, but how many are actually qualified? Are those who are qualified getting the attention warranted? In addition to feature writing, you can expect a scope of Business, Diet, Education, Politics, Local, National and International news.

✦ **FREE BUSINESS LISTING IN MTTB**
When traveling, how convenient it would be to find the kinds of quality products and services that you want while simultaneously recycling those dollars.

✦ **FREE PREPUBLISHING DISCOUNTS**
We will are always working on new books which are designed and compiled solely from the database of Messenger Elijah Muhammad. We will forward our members a discount off the publisher's price, and the member can use their member "discount off book" to realize even more savings!

✦ **20% DISCOUNT ON AUDIO TAPES**
Regardless where you may find audio tapes by Elijah Muhammad, you will pay at least $8 to $10 for a single 30 minute radio broadcast. Why bother? Our tapes are by far the best quality you can buy, because of our exclusive filtering, noise reduction process we subject all our tapes to. Now you can get good quality at a good low price.

✦ **20% DISCOUNT ON VIDEO TAPES**
Our list of video are of good quality. The events on the videos are from lectures and conventions which are rare and hard to come by.

✦ **20% DISCOUNT ON PHOTOGRAPHS**
Some of these photos and prints are rare photos, all of which are of Messenger Elijah Muhammad. The majority are black and white; however, we have color and duo-tones.

✦ **20% DISCOUNT ON ALL BOOKS BY ELIJAH MUHAMMAD**
We carry the classics such as Message To The Blackman In America, The Fall of America, How To Eat To Live - Books 1&2, Our Saviour Has Arrived, The Supreme Wisdom - Vol. 1 & 2, The Flag of Islam. NEW BOOKS: The Mother Plane, 100 Answers To The Most Uncomman 100 Questions, Jesus' History-His Birth & Death, History of The Nation of Islam, The Time & The Judgement, The Secrets of Freemasonry, Christianity vs Islam. (All perfect bound, gloss covered books) **AND YES - THE TRUE HISTORY OF MASTER FARD MUHAMMAD & THE TRUE HISTORY OF ELIJAH MUHAMMAD,** *AUTOBIOGRAPHICALLY AUTHORITATIVE*

FACTS

The National Survey reveals that the average audio tape of Elijah Muhmammd (30 minutes) will cost you approximately $8.00 or more!

Not only are our tapes of equal length as low as $6.95, BUT with a membership discount of 20% off, you only pay a low $5.56 - over 30% lower than anywhere in the country!!!

~ ~ ~

We send our tapes through a graphic equalizing and noise reduction process to eliminate unwanted hiss and noise. Why?

~ ~ ~

We're designed to do one thing - very well!

MEMPS MEMBERSHIP

Now Only

$30.00 per year!

You will save over $20 to $30 alone on just one purchase! The same $20 or so you would have spent elsewhere. Invest that extra cost in a membership and never worry about high prices again!

Please put me on your membership list for ______ MEMPS membership.
I have enclosed $ _________ and you may mail it to:

Name ______________________________

Address ______________________________

City ______________________________

State ________ Zip ____________ Phone ______________

Only $30 **per year**

Send payment to:

MEMPS P.O. Box 162412 • Atlanta, GA 30321

WHY NOW IS A GOOD TIME TO BECOME A MEMEBER?

- **First Automated Fax Retrieval of Elijah Muhammad Documents**
- **First Comprehensive Concordance**
- **First Comprehensive Subject Index**
- **First Alphabetized Anthology of Elijah Muhammad**
- **Many Specialized Research Compilations**
- **Lots, lots more . . . .**

These Powerful Research Projects Will Be Offered To The Public For The First Time!

Now Is The Time To Become A Member Before Membership Fees Increase!